Garter
and Ribbon
Snake Care

For Jenny

Quick & Easy Garter and Ribbon Snake Care

Project Team
Editor: Tom Mazorlig
Copy Editor: Carl Schutt
Design: Patricia Escabi
Series Design: Mary Ann Kahn

T.F.H. Publications
President/CEO: Glen S. Axelrod
Executive Vice President: Mark E. Johnson
Publisher: Christopher T. Reggio
Production Manager: Kathy Bontz

T.F.H. Publications, Inc.
One TFH Plaza
Third and Union Avenues
Neptune City, NJ 07753

Copyright © 2005 by T.F.H. Publications, Inc.

Library of Congress Cataloging-in-Publication Data
Purser, Phillip.
Quick and easy garter and ribbon snake care / Phillip Purser.
p. cm.
Includes index.
ISBN 0-7938-1023-X (alk. paper)
 1. Garter snakes. 2. Snakes as pets. 3. Captive snakes. I. Title.
SF459.S5P87 2005
639.3'962—dc22
2005012995

This book has been published with the intent to provide accurate and authoritative information in regard to the subject matter within. While every precaution has been taken in preparation of this book, the author and publisher expressly disclaim responsibility for any errors, omissions, or adverse effects arising from the use or application of the information contained herein. The techniques and suggestions are used at the reader's discretion and are not to be considered a substitute for veterinary care. If you suspect a medical problem, consult your veterinarian.

The Leader In Responsible Animal Care For Over 50 Years!™
www.tfhpublications.com

Table of Contents

Introducing Garter and Ribbon Snakes

Easily among the most popularly kept snakes in the world today, garter snakes and ribbon snakes have long been appreciated by European hobbyists but are only now coming into their own here in the United States. In years past, however, these demure serpents were overlooked by American reptile keepers—sold by mail order in the back of comic books and passed off by serious enthusiasts as snakes fit only to be kept by children. While garter snakes and ribbon snakes, with their gentle natures and hearty appetites, can make an excellent first pet snake for a child, they certainly have a lot to offer to hobbyists of all ages and experience levels.

Garter snakes and ribbon snakes are nonvenomous, relatively small snakes that are easily handled, seldom bite, and seem to enjoy the stimulation and warmth of gentle handling more so than many other snakes. Junior hobbyists and budding enthusiasts can hone their serpent-keeping skills with a garter or ribbon snake, while advanced hobbyists can successfully breed the garter or ribbon snakes in captivity with minimal difficulty.

Every year these species appear on the pet trade in larger and larger numbers and in increasingly diverse and interesting varieties. While the most attractive of these garter snakes, such as the albino or flame-red varieties or the rare San Francisco garter snake, may demand a high price, the lion's share of garter and ribbon snakes can be purchased at a very reasonable cost.

Found throughout virtually all of North America and south to Honduras in Central America, the garter snakes and ribbon snakes occur wherever the environment will support them. They thrive in fields, wooded lowlands, streamside forests, swamps, and other such areas where prey (earthworms, slugs, frogs, toads, and fish) abounds. Ribbon snakes, being the more aquatic of the two, are seldom

Relationships

The garter snakes and ribbon snakes belong to the family Colubridae, which is composed of over 2,500 species, making it the largest family of snakes in the world. Snakes of this family are called colubrids. Identifiable by their rough texture (owing to their keeled scales), slim bodies, large eyes, agility, and skeletal similarities, the garter and ribbon snakes are further divided into the genus *Thamnophis*, which is Latin, meaning "shrub-snake" or "snake of the bushes," in reference to these species' propensity for climbing and hunting amidst low-growing vegetation.

Each scale on the back and sides of garter and ribbon snakes has a keel, giving the snake a rough texture. Red-spotted garter snake pictured.

encountered far from a permanent source of water. Garter snakes, however, may be found in virtually any environment within their natural range. Frequently encountered by exploring children, garter snakes are often found prowling through flowerbeds, slinking about backyard shrubs, and gliding through vegetable gardens—a practice that has earned this species the colloquial name "garden snake."

Most garter and ribbon snakes have adapted to a climate consisting of short summers and long, cold winters. They bear live young, unlike most other snakes that lay eggs, because the warm seasons were not long enough to accommodate months of egg incubation. If the young are to survive, they have to get as early a start as possible. They have a number of other adaptations to a climate with a long cold season, including the ability to hibernate for long periods—some species can even freeze solid and emerge in the spring none the worse for the wear. Even today the cold-tolerant eastern garter snake is one of the few snake species known to exist within the Arctic Circle.

Introducing Garter and Ribbon Snakes

Scientific Names

You may have noticed that sometimes there are words in italics that appear after the name of an animal. This is the scientific name, and each animal only has one scientific name. Biologists determine the scientific name of each animal based on what other animals it is related to. The first part of the name is called the *genus*. The second part is the *species*, and this combination of genus and species is unique for each animal. Sometimes, there is a third name. This is the subspecies, a name given to groups of animals that are the same species, but that do have some differences between them. Not all species have subspecies.

The reason scientific names exist is so that scientists all over the world can talk about each animal without worrying about language barriers or other similar animals being confused with the one they want to discuss. The scientific name for the common garter snake is *Thamnophis sirtalis* and the name for the eastern ribbon snake is *Thamnophis sauritis*. Both species also have subspecies.

If you use the genus name once, you can abbreviate it to the first letter when you write about it later. So, if I was talking about garter snakes again, I could just type *T. sirtalis*. Also, if I wanted to talk about all the snakes in the same genus as the garter snakes, I would just say *Thamnophis*.

If you decide to do more reading about keeping pet reptiles and amphibians, you should become accustomed to scientific names, since authors and hobbyists use them frequently.

Getting One

Because of their popularity in the pet trade, garter and ribbon snakes are often easily acquired species. The hobbyist may purchase one from a local pet shop, from an online retailer, at a reptile expo, or, in some cases, may capture his or her own pet from the wild. Special

Quick & Easy Garter and Ribbon Snake Care

precautions must be taken, however, in collecting your own pet garter or ribbon snake from the wild. Local, state, and federal laws protect these snakes from collection, molestation, and harassment throughout much of the United States. The San Francisco garter snake, for example, is federally protected throughout its entire range. Anyone found collecting this species without proper licensing is subject to fines and possibly even imprisonment.

Take the time to study all laws and ordinances that might affect your area before you hit the woods in search of a pet garter snake. Other drawbacks to collecting a garter snake from the wild is that not only do you deplete the wild population of garter snakes by removing an animal from his home ecosystem, but the chances are any snake you capture will suffer from heavy parasite loads (worms, protozoa, ticks, and mites), which will involve serious veterinary treatment to correct.

Reptile Expos
Attending a reptile expo is a good way to obtain a pet garter or ribbon snake. Reptile expos (or herp shows, as they are often called) involve large numbers of professional breeders gathering together in

Herp Is the Word

Throughout this book, you will see the term *herps*. This word refers both reptiles and amphibians together. This word comes from the word *herpetology*, which is the study of reptiles and amphibians. When speaking of the hobby of keeping reptiles and amphibians, you can call it the *herp hobby*. *Herpetoculture* is the keeping and breeding of reptiles and amphibians. A *herper* is some one who participates in the herp hobby or herpetoculture (also called a *herp hobbyist*).

These terms are handy to know, not just for reading this book, but because you will see them in other herp publications and on the Internet, and hear other hobbyists use these words.

a coliseum, conference center, farmer's market, or other large building. These dealers set up their finest stock on tables, offering their best animals at reasonable prices. If you're as big a fan of reptiles and amphibians as I am, you'll feel like a kid in a candy store when you attend a reptile expo. Table after table after table awaits you; each one teeming with deli cups and terrariums filled with slithering or crawling cold-blooded delights. Because garter snakes are so popular in the pet trade, you're likely to find at least one or two dealers specializing in these snakes.

The only drawback to purchasing your garter or ribbon snake at a reptile expo is that all sales are final. Since the expo will end so soon, there is no way any of the dealers can offer a return policy on an animal that expires soon after purchase. A second trap to be wary of at a reptile expo is dealers trading illegally collected animals. These poachers will be offering animals at very low prices, and chances are your animal will be highly stressed (captured, housed under insufficient conditions, and brought to market) and will likely suffer from internal and external parasites. Unlike most dealers you will encounter at a reptile expo, poachers are irresponsible, uncaring people who deal in reptiles just to get some fast cash. Make sure that any garter or ribbon snake you purchase is from a well-known, reputable dealer.

Albino checkered garter snakes are captive bred in decent numbers. Albino individuals usually cost more than normal ones.

Online Vendors

Online purchases are very similar to purchasing your pet at a reptile expo. While you do not have the opportunity to physically inspect the animal you intend to purchase, you do get the peace of mind when purchasing from the web site of a professional breeder. Professional breeders are men and women who have dedicated their lives to raising healthy and beautiful reptiles and amphibians. E-mailed photos and detailed descriptions of any snakes you are interested in are free for the asking from a professional breeder's site. These breeders know that their business hinges on providing the best possible animal to the customer, and, as a result, most breeders will go the extra mile in caring for their customers. Unlike reptile expos, however, most breeders will offer a return or exchange policy on their livestock.

Because a professional breeder dealing in garter and ribbon snakes is so skilled at keeping and raising these reptiles, he or she can function as a well of knowledge, answering any questions you might have and offering their expertise whenever they can. Of course, you'll pay a little more money for an animal raised by a conscientious, professional breeder, but the quality of the animal you will receive and the customer care that often accompanies such a purchase are well worth the price. Professional breeders can be a source of rare, unique, or hard-to-find varieties of garter and ribbon snakes.

Pet Stores

The final option of obtaining a garter or ribbon snake is through your local pet shop. The main advantages to purchasing your pet snake from a local shop is that you have the ability to thoroughly inspect any animal you are interested in before making a purchase and are close to the source of your animal should something go wrong. Of course, there are also drawbacks to purchasing from a local pet shop. Oftentimes, the staff of such a shop is less than knowledgeable about garter and ribbon snakes. If the clerk who sells you the snake is an expert in parrots or in marine fish, he or she may not be able to answer all your reptile related questions. If at all possible, conduct your business with the store's reptile expert. If he or she is not present the day you come in, ask when would be a better time to speak with him or her and come back then. Because the initial purchase of your garter or ribbon snake is easily the most critical step in your pet snake endeavor, you'll certainly want to do all you can to ensure the animal you purchase is as healthy and hardy as possible.

Selecting a Healthy Snake

By following the guidelines listed below, you can ensure that the garter or ribbon snake that you purchase is as healthy as possible.

The first thing to look for is the cleanliness of the terrarium in which the garter snakes are housed. Under ideal conditions, the terrarium will be clean (in appearance and smell) and populated by only a few snakes. Each animal should have a hiding spot, there should be plenty of artificial foliage, and the terrarium should be equipped with one or more dishes of clean, fresh water. If the terrarium is filthy, smells foul, or is overcrowded with a dozen or more snakes, then the wise hobbyist will recognize these warning signs and stay away. Purchasing an animal from such a filthy environment is never a good idea, as continued exposure to feces, urine, and high levels of stress will soon take its toll on these animals, making them very prone to infection and ailment.

If the pet shop's terrarium is clean, and each animal has a hiding place, then you'll want to move on to the behavior tests. All species of garter and ribbon snakes are naturally highly alert and sometimes jumpy animals. They have superior eyesight, so when you approach the terrarium any snakes that can see you should immediately react. Snakes that are drinking or basking may retreat into hiding, or they may freeze-up, tensing their muscles and staring at you while sitting completely motionless. In the wild, garter and ribbon snakes will

Many garter and ribbon snakes (eastern ribbon snake pictured here) dwell near water and are excellent swimmers.

defend themselves by remaining perfectly still when a predator draws near, hoping to remain unseen. A specimen that does not react to your presence (seems too relaxed, lays outstretched, takes no notice of you at all) may not be in the best health. Sickly or ailing animals are often too weak to react as they naturally would if they were in peak health.

Now it's time to move on to the physical inspection. Gently lift your chosen garter snake out of the terrarium. Does he try to get away? Does he musk, bite, or exude his waste products on you (gross, I know, but it's one of their natural defenses)? Whatever his reaction, a healthy garter or ribbon snake will do *something* when you pick him up. An animal that lays limp in your hands or that does not move at all is seriously ill and should never be purchased. Handle the snake for a while to determine his disposition. If he continues to bite/musk, then he may only be frightened at the moment, or he may be a more aggressive or nervous individual. Such a high-strung animal may never tame to handling, and may also be too nervous in the home terrarium to ever eat properly. A stressed snake would sooner starve to death than eat in an uncomfortable situation. If, however, the snake calms and rests or slithers quietly through your fingers, then he is demonstrating the most desirable disposition of all. A garter or ribbon snake that is this calm will make an excellent pet that you will be able

Choose a pet snake that is alert and attentive; a listless one may be ill. This is a healthy eastern garter snake.

to handle. He will also likely adapt very quickly and thoroughly to the sights and smells of his new terrarium once you get him home.

Now it's time to inspect the snake for injuries or parasites. Look the entire animal over very carefully. Are there any open wounds, sores, lesions, blisters, pustules, or patches of discolored or misshapen scales? Do you see any bumps or plump protuberances around the snake's eyes, mouth or cloaca (these are ticks, and will be dark brown, reddish brown, or black in color)? Is the belly of the garter snake flat and smooth, or is it sunken in (a sign of malnutrition)? Any irregularities in the skin such as wounds or sores, or any ticks present are definite signs of poor health.

Next, wet a white paper towel (must be totally white, no dyes or patterns), place it on the palm of your hand, grip the snake gently behind the head, and wipe the paper towel down the length of the snake's body. Repeat this act, making sure the wet paper towel touches the garter or ribbon snake on all surfaces. Now look at the paper towel. A healthy specimen will leave nothing behind on the paper towel. An ailing snake, however, may leave behind numerous black or gray-red flecks. These flecks are mites, which are insidious, blood-sucking parasites. If mites are present on your chosen garter snake, put the animal back and do not purchase him, or any other snakes from that terrarium. Mites are prolific and can infect an entire collection of reptiles in a short period of time. Purchasing a mite-infested animal is a bad idea.

A final measure of inspection that you may want to conduct in the pet shop is to witness your chosen animal feed. Even the healthiest of garter snakes will not stay that way for long if he does not feed in captivity. Normally, healthy garter and ribbon snakes have hearty appetites and, once they realize prey is in the area, will attack with gusto, often swallowing their prey while it is still alive. A captive garter snake—if he is healthy and has adapted well to captive life—should display no less fervor at the dinner table.

Lastly, if the garter or ribbon snake you are interested in purchasing is housed alone, you may wish to inspect that animal's stool. Healthy stool samples will be moist but should have definite form. Snake feces are dark brown to black, and are typically excreted in conjunction with a whitish to yellow granular paste, which is actually the snake's urine. Excessively runny, bloody, or intensely sweet smelling feces is a sign that your chosen snake has some internal infection and will not likely stay in peak health for long. Do not purchase an animal that displays irregular stool.

Prerequisite to actually purchasing the snake, however, is the establishment of a home terrarium in which the animal will be housed. It is never a good idea to purchase your snake, terrarium, and décor all in one day. Have your terrarium set up before you purchase your snake. Leaving your garter or ribbon snake waiting around in a cold, dark box for an hour or more while you set up his habitat will cause the animal undue stress and can weaken his immune system. A quick, smooth transition from the pet shop to a warm, secure terrarium is definitely the way to go.

The only major drawback to keeping garter and ribbon snakes is their rel-atively short lifespans. Other colubrid snakes, such

A northwestern garter snake holds the record for being the oldest known garter snake; one lived to be 16 years old.

Introducing Garter and Ribbon Snakes

Names List

Here is a list of the common and scientific names of the garter and ribbon snakes illustrated in this book.

Blue-striped Garter, *T. sirtalis similis* (pg. 3)
Blue-striped Ribbon, *T. sauritus nitae*
Butler's Garter, *T. butleri*
Checkered Garter, *T. marcianus* (pg. 4)
Coast Garter, *T. elegans terrestris*
Eastern Black-necked Garter, *T. cyrtopsis ocellatus*
Eastern Garter, *T. sirtalis sirtalis*
Eastern Ribbon, *T. sauritus sauritus*
Gulf Coast Ribbon, *T. proximus orarius*
Northwestern Garter, *T. ordinoides*
Peninsula Ribbon, *T. sauritus sackeni*
Red-sided Garter, *T. sirtalis parietalis*
Red-spotted Garter, *T. sirtalis concinnus*
Red-striped Ribbon, *T. proximus rubrilineatus*
San Francisco Garter, *T. sirtalis tetrataenia*
Two-striped Garter, *T. hammondi*
Valley Garter, *T. sirtalis fitchi* (pg. 1)
Wandering Garter, *T. elegans vagrans*
Western Black-necked Garter, *T. cyrtopsis cyrtopsis*

as the rat snakes and the king snakes, may live more than 25 years in the captive environment. The garter snakes, however, seldom exceed 10 years old. The oldest known garter snake was a northwestern garter snake, *T. ordinoides*, which lived to be an astonishing 16 years old. Even when housed under nearly perfect conditions, the short-lived ribbon snakes rarely reach five to six years old. While it is certain that no hobbyist wants to say good-bye to his or her beloved pet, these species' shorter life spans must be taken into account before purchasing a garter or ribbon snake. Most hobbyists agree that a keeper-kept relationship with a garter or ribbon snake should stress pleasurable handling, enjoyable observation, and quality time over quantity of years.

Garter and Ribbon Snake Housing

When it comes to housing garter and ribbon snakes, the hobbyist's options are many. Garter and ribbon snakes will thrive in habitats ranging from the most elaborate living vivarium, complete with live plants and flowing water falls, to the simplest terrariums floored in a substrate of white paper towels and outfitted with only the necessities. Ease of housing is, in fact, one of the major contributing factors to these snakes' overwhelming popularity worldwide. These snakes are so adaptable and forgiving in their needs for housing that enthusiasts at all points of the experience continuum can successfully house a garter or ribbon snake.

Quarantine

It is highly recommended that you have two cages at home, both of which will function as homes for your garter or ribbon snake. The first one is the quarantine tank. Sparsely outfitted with only the bare necessities, the quarantine tank is a home designed for the observation and isolation of your new garter or ribbon snake. For at least the first two weeks after bringing him home, you will watch your new pet closely, observing for any signs of illness. If you will eventually be bringing your garter or ribbon snake into the same room with a larger reptile or amphibian collection, quarantine should last for one or two months.

To construct the quarantine tank, you'll want to begin with a clean, 10- to 30-gallon-sized glass aquarium placed in a room far away from any other reptile or amphibian pets you may own, so as to prevent the spread of any disease your new pet may be carrying. Cover the floor of the aquarium with several layers of white paper towel. Atop this paper towel substrate, place a hide box and a water dish, and a climbing branch. Maintain temperatures of 79° to 82° Fahrenheit in the quarantine tank, with a basking spot of 85° to 88°F (see section on heating for details on maintaining this temperature).

The philosophy behind the quarantine tank is that the snake must have some place in which he can hide and feel secure but must not be able to escape the view of his keeper, who will daily monitor him

No Ink

If you are using paper towels as the substrate for your quarantine tank, do not use paper towels with dyes or inks in them, as these inks may be harmful to your snake. You can also use the plain brown, recycled paper towels, although the brown color makes it slightly more difficult to see if there is anything abnormal about the feces.

Potting soil is an acceptable substrate for a garter or ribbon snake terrarium, but do not allow it to become soggy. A Butler's garter snake is pictured.

for signs of illness or infection. By outfitting with only one hide box, the keeper ensures that there will be no difficulty in locating the garter or ribbon snake when the time comes to physically inspect the animal. Because the terrarium is floored in white paper towels, the hobbyist can easily monitor for the presence of mites (tiny, dark flecks seen crawling along the paper towel) as well as for runny or bloody stool, which will readily be seen against the white paper towel backdrop.

The Permanent Home

After quarantine is over, you'll want to transfer your snake to a permanent terrarium. Outfit the floor of this terrarium with an organic mulch or bedding. I recommend using shredded coconut husks, bark-chips, or one of the many "forest mix" beddings that are available at your local pet shop. Fertilizer-free potting soil is also an excellent option. Cedar chips and pine shavings must be avoided at all costs, however, as these scented materials contain heavy resins that are dangerous and sometimes fatal to garter/ribbon snakes.

When constructing the permanent terrarium, keep the snake's genus name in mind: *Thamnophis* means "snake of the bushes."

Garter and Ribbon Snake Housing   19

The Aquaterrarium

Most species of garter and ribbon snakes will thrive in a aquaterrarium, which is half-land and half-water. Aquarterrariums employ a great many natural components so as to make a virtual ecosystem for the inhabitants. Construct a aquarterrarium by installing a commercially available aquarterrarium-conversion kit or by sealing a plexiglas divider in the middle of your terrarium. Fill one half of the tank with dry substrate (potting soil, if you are going to have live plants in the land section), and fill the other with water. By employing underwater filters, water lettuce, and water hyacinth, you can sustain a perfectly clean and thriving aquatic system within the aquarterrarium, while also employing live plants in the deep substrate of the dry half of the aquarterrarium. Aquarterrariums are best for the common garter snake and its subspecies, as well as the eastern and blue-striped ribbon snake. Make sure that ventilation in the aquarterrarium is superior, as humidity can quickly build up inside the tank and become problematic for your snake.

Your new friend will need to climb and hide amidst foliage. Most hobbyists prefer using artificial plants to live ones, as artificial plants are easily cleaned, will never die, and do not need to be watered or maintained like live plants. Employ artificial plants at all levels of the terrarium. Place ferns and grasses on the floor of the tank, attach (via their suction cups) broad-leafed plants on the walls of the terrarium, and weave artificial vines throughout the tank. Giving your garter or ribbon snake plenty of green, leafy cover in which to hunt, hide, or simply hang out is an excellent practice that will keep your new pet happy and stress free.

Despite the amount of foliage you employ in the terrarium, ground-level hides are also important. Garter and ribbon snakes, like most snakes, need a dark, secure place in which to retreat. Commercially available hide boxes and artificial (polymer) log-halves are both excellent choices, as they afford deep, dark seclusion for your snake, and they are easily removed for cleaning. When purchasing a hide, remember that the feeling of security comes only when the snake's body touches his enclosure on all sides. A hide, therefore, must be the right size to accommodate your pet. Avoid purchasing very large or cavernous hides for smaller snakes, as these items will not afford your snake the snug, secure feeling he desires.

In nature, neither garter snakes nor ribbon snakes thrive far from a permanent source of water. A large water dish, therefore, is a necessity in the captive environment. Make sure that the dish is neither too deep nor escape-proof. Even though garter and ribbon snakes are superior swimmers, they can quickly exhaust themselves and drown in a dish from which they cannot escape. Employ shallow dishes or extend branches into the dish so that a trapped snake can simply climb out to freedom.

Speaking of freedom, there is certainly no room for "freedom" when it comes to the security of your snake's terrarium. Proving themselves masters of escape time and time again, both garter and ribbon snakes are adept at finding and squeezing through even the tiniest gaps in their terrarium. Finding a lid that fits snugly and securely, therefore, is paramount. Use a lid that fastens, locks, or otherwise secures tightly to the top of your terrarium.

Humidity

Proper air circulation is a must in the snake's terrarium, for while these species naturally frequent moist areas, a saturated atmosphere or excessively damp substrate will quickly prove

Peninsula ribbon snakes and the other snakes discussed here will climb branches in nature and should be supplied with climbing areas in captivity.

problematic to these snakes' health. By the same token, too little humidity can also be a problem. The trick to balancing humidity is to understand the natural environment from which your chosen species of garter or ribbon snake comes, and do your best to simulate those conditions in captivity. Lower the humidity in your terrarium by adding a circulation fan atop the lid or by using drier substrate. Conversely, you can increase humidity levels by placing an extra water dish in the terrarium. As the water evaporates, it will make the air in the terrarium more humid and conducive to healthy sheds among many humidity-loving species. Monitor humidity by placing a humidity gauge in the center of the inside-back wall of the terrarium.

Heating

While garter and ribbon snakes are cold tolerant, this in no way suggests that they do not require ample amounts of heat in the captive environment. In nature, snakes warm themselves by basking in the early morning sunlight. When they get warm enough, they will hunt, and when their body grows uncomfortably warm, snakes will retreat to a cool, dark place to cool down; a process known as behavioral thermoregulation (controlling temperature through behavior).

To create a basking spot in the terrarium, you may wish to take either the heat lamp route or the heating pad route. If you opt for the lamp route, place an incandescent fixture atop the terrarium, and use a 60 to 75 watt light bulb—or higher wattage for a large terrarium. Adding a florescent fixture atop your terrarium is an excellent idea for viewing your snake. Florescent lights cast a lot of light, but in a well-ventilated terrarium, they generate virtually no additional heat.

If you opt for the heating pad route to thermoregulation, you will want to place an undertank heating pad (which adheres to the *outside* of the terrarium) to the bottom of the terrarium. Spread the substrate of the terrarium fairly thin directly above the heating pad, so that your pet may absorb as much heat as he desires in a short amount of time.

In either case, heat lamp or heating pad, make sure to only place your heating apparatus at one end of the tank. Your garter or ribbon snake must be able to retreat away from his heat source when he needs to. Animals that cannot escape their basking area can overheat and die in a matter of minutes. Suitable ambient temperature in the terrarium is 74° to 83°F, while the basking spot should not exceed 87° to 88°F. Turning off your heat lamp or unplugging your heating pad at night, such that your terrarium will experience a temperature drop of five to seven degrees is a sound practice, as this nightly drop will help to maintain your snake's natural metabolism and bodily processes.

Maintanence

Cleaning and maintaining the snake's terrarium is seldom a problem. As you notice feces or other wastes in the tank, remove them (and the immediately surrounding substrate) promptly. Once every few weeks, remove any and all inhabitants from the terrarium and break the terrarium down for a thorough cleaning. Dispose of all substrate, wash all cage furnishings in hot, soapy water, and wash the terrarium itself in a bath of warm, soapy water. A mild, antibacterial soap is ideal for this purpose, as it will kill a wide variety of microbes and rinses clean away. Never clean your snake's terrarium with harsh, odorific cleansers, as these chemical agents can pose serious risks to your snake's skin, olfactory glands, and

Hot Rocks Are Bad

Avoid using heating rocks or other heating apparatus inside the terrarium. Not only are heating rocks dangerous but their cord must run out of the terrarium to the wall outlet, leaving a gap between the lid and the terrarium through which your garter or ribbon snake could easily escape. Hot rocks can easily trap a small snake underneath and cook him; additionally they have been known to develop spots that are much hotter than normal, creating a burn hazard.

general health. Pay special attention to the water dishes used in the terrarium, as these items will likely harbor the most bacteria and fungi of all. Scrub your snake's water dish as you would your own coffee mug or favorite cup. Within my own collection, I simply rotate out water dishes, removing the old one to the dishwasher and replacing it with a clean one.

During this period of intense cleaning, you might want to inspect your snake for any signs of ill health. Give the animal a gentle once-over while his terrarium is drying. If the terrarium is particularly filthy (sometimes captive snakes may slither through their own wastes), you might want to bathe your garter snake. Bathing consists of letting the snake swim about (under your careful supervision) in a shallow tub of lukewarm water for about 10 minutes. Once you've washed and thoroughly rinsed all items and the terrarium, and they have dried out, replace all items, floor the terrarium with fresh substrate, and return your pet snake to his freshly cleaned home.

Handling

Handling your garter or ribbon snake can be a fun and rewarding experience, but certain precautions must be taken to ensure that neither you, nor your pet, are harmed during the experience. Humans have more strength in their grasp than we may realize, and since our hands are a lot tougher than a garter/ribbon snake's spine and rib cage, we must take care in picking up and handling our snakes.

When you remove your snake from his terrarium, try to coax the animal into slithering into your palm, and then lift him gently out, making sure to support his body weight evenly in your hands. Carelessly grabbing a garter or ribbon snake can seriously damage the animal's vertebrae, skeleton, and nervous system. Never squeeze your garter snake or hold him with a closed fist. Instead, let the animal roam freely from one hand to the other unrestrained. Grasping a garter or ribbon snake near his head or near his tail will very likely upset the animal, causing him to thrash and attempt to escape, which may also lead to unexpectedly negative results. A struggling snake may inadvertently injure himself or bite his keeper. It is always important, therefore, that your snake feel safe and secure in your hands, never constrained or threatened. Very young hobbyists should never handle a snake unsupervised. If all goes well, your snake will enjoy the gentle warmth of your touch, while you relish the interesting movements, unblinking stare, and mysterious nature of your scaly friend.

Once handling time is over, return your snake to his terrarium, carefully letting him slither out of your hands and back into his

Living Together

Garter and ribbon snakes are docile animals that may be housed together in communal terrariums. If you decide to keep multiple animals in the same tank, make sure that each one has plenty of hides and space to roam; house at densities of no more than one snake per ten gallons of terrarium space. It is important that each snake get enough to eat when housed communally. If one snake in the terrarium has a dominant disposition, he is likely to eat more than his fair share of food.

Most garter and ribbon snakes will become used to gentle handling and become quite tame. A red-sided garter snake is pictured.

habitat. Now that the snake has suffered no ill effects from handling, let's be sure you don't either. As much as we may love and enjoy our reptilian pets, the reality of life is that these animals can harbor bacteria on their bodies that may be harmful to us as humans. Snakes living in filthy conditions are *far more likely* to harbor dangerous pathogens, such as *Salmonella*, but even the cleanest snake terrarium is not guaranteed to be safe. Immediately after handling your garter/ribbon snake, wash and scrub your hands (up to the elbow) with hot water and antibacterial soap. You must never rub your eyes or eat while handling your pet snake, nor should you handle a second pet snake before washing up after handling the first.

Washing your hands is the most important step in preventing contamination of any kind. Of course, the inverse of this is also true; just as you might get sick from handling a filthy snake, a snake might get sick from being handled by a filthy keeper! Perfumes, cleansers, nail polishes, cooking oil, and a host of other household chemicals that we come into contact with every day can prove dangerous to your garter snake. Make sure to always wash and rinse your hand thoroughly *before* handling your pet snake.

Feeding Your Snake

Feeding time in the garter snake terrarium is always fun, unless, of course, you're the food item! Garter and ribbon snakes are neither constrictors, nor are they venomous, so their only means of dispatching prey is to swallow it as quickly as possible, most often while the prey is still alive. This feat requires speed, agility, and dexterity on the part of the snake, and makes for quite the interesting display in captivity. Even when dining on nonliving food items, these snakes tend to display excessive enthusiasm: twisting, turning, and raising a general ruckus while consuming their meal.

As you might have suspected, garter and ribbon snakes are carnivores that favor prey items found in and around permanent waterways, including minnows, frogs, tadpoles, salamanders, earthworms, slugs, and occasionally small mammals. In nature, a garter snake may consume, albeit rarely, small amphiumas and sirens, freshwater eels, and recently molted crayfish. Fortunately, garter and ribbon snakes do not need a perfectly simulated natural diet to thrive in captivity. All the items they need to live may be purchased from your local pet store or bait shop.

Fish

Fish comprise the lion's share of most garter and ribbon snakes' diets. Place living feeder goldfish, guppies, tuffies, or bait shop minnows in your snake's water dish, and let the snake feed at his leisure. A debate has arisen in recent years as to whether goldfish supply a garter or ribbon snake with sufficient nutrients. Some experts say yes, and some

Controversial Goldfish

Feeding feeder goldfish to snakes, frogs, cichlids, and other animals has started to come under fire from hobbyists, herpetologists, and ichthyologists. One reason is that feeder goldfish are kept in crowded, often filthy conditions at many wholesalers and pet stores. Because of this, they can be diseased or carry parasites. Another reason some experts denounce the feeding of feeder goldfish to other animals is that they cause thiamin deficiency. This seems to be true most often when goldfish—especially frozen goldfish—make up the major part of the diet.

However, many keepers feed their snakes feeder goldfish and do not experience any problems. It is possible that feeding feeder goldfish to your snakes poses no risk. If you want to be totally certain that you are not exposing your pet to feeder goldfish-caused illness, you can buy frozen whole fish (usually silversides) in most pet stores. These do not carry parasites. To prevent thiamine deficiency, feed a variety of prey to your snake.

Garter and ribbon snakes, like this northwestern garter, relish chunks of fish, but the snakes require a varied diet.

say no. Perhaps the best solution to the problem is to offer a mixture of fish types, which will help ensure your garter snake is receiving the nutrients he needs. One week, feed goldfish, the next feed guppies, the next feed minnows, etc.

If the snake is hungry, he will quickly slither into the dish, hold his mouth agape, and swish his head around underwater until he catches a fish. With his inward curving teeth and powerful jaws, a garter snake seldom drops a fish once he has snagged one. The garter or ribbon snake will then swallow the fish by working his jaws forward over his victim in a side-to-side motion.

Although some experts advise feeding cut strips of frozen fish (catfish, whitefish, or tilapia) to garter/ribbon snakes, I must disagree with this practice. While most captive garters will greedily accept strips of raw catfish, this meal cannot come close to providing all the necessary nutrients that garter and ribbon snakes need to thrive and grow. Strips of fish provide mostly protein (in the form of muscle-meat), and rob the snake of vital vitamins and minerals found in the brains, organs, and bones of a whole fish. Whenever possible, feed your garter or ribbon snake whole fish, and not strips of fish muscle-meat.

I have also found that offering more, smaller feeders is preferable to offering fewer, larger prey items. Garter and ribbon snakes seem more able to digest smaller prey items, and they may regurgitate large fishes. If consistently fed a diet of very large fish, which he must struggle to swallow, your snake risks damaging his esophagus and jaws.

Some individual garter snakes may also have the curious habit of gorging themselves when food is abundant, eating beyond their capacity and regurgitating most of their prey. Simply because your garter snake seems hungry or is patrolling the water dish looking for more prey does not mean you should feed him any more. Two to four appropriately sized minnows are enough for one sitting. After a few days, you can offer more. What is appropriately sized, you ask? The prey item should be small enough such that your garter can swallow it in less than one minute and it leaves only a slightly noticeable lump in your snake's belly. Fish that take several minutes to consume or which seriously stretch your snake's body are too large.

Earthworms

Earthworms are another excellent feeder item that may be purchased easily and inexpensively. To feed an earthworm to your pet snake, simply wriggle the worm about in front of the snake. If your pet is overly enthusiastic, you might want to use feeding tongs or place the worm on a flat rock or small dish in the terrarium to keep from being bitten by a hungry garter snake. If, on the other hand, your snake is very shy (ribbon snakes are typically much shier than garters), you may need to place the earthworm in a shallow dish, angle the dish near the ribbon snake's retreat, and leave the room. If frightened or uncomfortable, a snake will not dine, no matter how tempting the meal might be.

Another reason to hand-feed earthworms or place them on a smooth surface, is that when frightened or attacked, earthworms will secrete thick fluids that will cause dirt, soil, and other bits of substrate to adhere to the worm. As the garter snake consumes the dirt-covered worm, it will likely ingest the bits of dirt. Continued ingesting of earth over the long-term can cause serious intestinal blockage and may lead to future health problems in your garter snake.

Leeches

Some species of *Thamnophis*, the ribbon snakes in particular, are fond of leeches. Purchase these bloodsucking invertebrates at local bait shops or from specialty online retailers. While your garter or ribbon snake may find a leech a tasty meal, these worms are not the most nutritious of feeders, and should only be offered as an occasional treat, not a staple.

Frogs

Frogs make great occasional supplements to the diet of large garter and ribbon snakes but should not be offered as a staple. Care should be taken when feeding frogs to your garter snake, too, as these amphibians can carry internal parasites that can infect your snake. Minimize the chances of this occurring by humanely pre-killing and then freezing the frog. The hobbyist should also take all necessary steps in determining what species of frog he or she is offering to his or her pet snake. While garter and ribbon snakes can readily consume green treefrogs (*Hyla cinerea*), gray treefrogs (*Hyla versicolor*), Cuban treefrogs (*Osteopilus septentrionalis*), and others, they are not equipped to digest the noxious toxins secreted by some frogs. The river frog (*Rana heckscheri*), for example, secretes a vile skin-toxin. Any snake that consumes a river frog will become violently ill for a day or longer.

Another drawback to feeding live frogs is that they don't simply lay down and die. When attacked by a hungry garter snake, most frogs will defend themselves by kicking, puffing up (making it difficult for the snake to swallow them), or even biting at your pet. Though you might not think it, many frog species have teeth, and when their life is in

Earthworms can be purchased at many pet stores and bait shops. They are nutritious and eagerly consumed by most garter and ribbon snakes.

danger, some of these little amphibians can draw blood from their attackers. Never feed live frogs to small or weak garter or ribbon snakes. Never feed any species of toad to your snake.

Tadpoles, which are also relished by the these serpents, are a far better choice as feeders than adult frogs. Not only are they less likely to transmit any bacteria or parasites to your snake, but they can also resist being eaten no more than a minnow can. Soft, plump, and nutritious, a tadpole makes a wonderful addition to your captive pet's diet. Simply drop the tadpole into a clean water dish just as you would a goldfish or minnow, and watch your snake go!

If unavailable in a pet shop, most bait shops are sure to have tadpoles in stock. Be aware, however, that tadpoles are rich in fats and proteins, and feeding too many to your garter snake will lead to obesity, thus significantly shortening your pet's life span.

Salamanders

Sometimes known as "spring lizards," these protein-rich amphibians come in a range of sizes and species to accommodate all variety of garter and ribbon snakes. The same rules of feeding frogs apply to the feeding of salamanders: feed only on occasion, never feed live salamanders (as they, too, carry parasites), and know what species of salamander you are feeding. The slimy salamander, *Plethodon glutinosus*, secretes a very sticky, foul tasting mucus-substance when molested. This noxious goo is thick enough to gum-up the mouth and throat of your garter snake, thus this species should never be offered as food. Salamanders hailing from the genus *Desmognathus*, however, make excellent meals for both garter and ribbon snakes. Do not exceed two salamander feedings a month. Check to make sure that collecting salamanders is legal in your area, and be sure you do not capture any threatened or endangered species.

Gut-Loading

Most feeder items are fed low-quality foods, thus they have little nutrients to offer your garter/ribbon snake. Make each meal more nutritious by gut-loading your feeders. House minnows, goldfish, guppies, and tadpoles in an interim aquarium for 48 hours before placing them in your snake's terrarium. During this time, feed them plenty of highly nutritious fish foods. The nutrients they ingest will benefit your snake when he dines on these gut-loaded feeder items.

Rodents

A final item that might make its way onto the garter snake's captive menu is the pinkie mouse. Consumed only by the largest of garter and ribbon snakes, pinkie mice are the tiny, hairless baby mice that are typically a week old or less when offered to a snake. Pinkies are high in protein and calcium but are also very rich in fats, which can prove problematic to your snake if fed too often. I recommend offering pinkie mice to your snake as an occasional treat, not as a regular food staple. An adult garter can take two pinkies per month without experiencing any ill effects of an improper diet. If you plan on breeding your garter snakes, then offering two pinkies a month to your female is an excellent way to condition her and prepare her for the rigors of reproduction.

Many garter and ribbon snakes feed heavily on amphibians—frogs and salamanders—in nature.

Adult checkered, blue-striped, common, and red-sided garter snakes are particularly known for consuming pinkies in captivity,

Because garter snakes normally dine on amphibian, fish, or invertebrate prey, they may need a little coaxing before taking a pinkie meal. Scenting is the act of rubbing a pinkie mouse against a pungent food item that your garter snakes already eats in order to trick the snake into eating the pinkie. Rub a slimy minnow, salamander, or earthworm against the pinkie mouse in order to transfer the scent just moments before offering the pinkie to your snake. If live prey items are unavailable for scenting, commercially manufactured scents may be purchased at your local pet shop. Simply spray or drip a small amount of the scent on the pinkie prior to presenting it to your garter snake.

Vitamin Supplements

While wild garter and ribbon snakes may take in all the necessary vitamins and minerals they need for growth, metabolism, and proper development, our captive friends seldom receive all the nutrients they need from their meals. Vitamin and mineral supplements, therefore, are a necessity of the captive diet. Most experts agree that dusting one meal a week with a reptile-specific multivitamin powder is sufficient. Vitamins should not be given too often, however, as vitamin toxicity may occur. Excess consumption of vitamin A can cause serious damage to the organs and nervous system of your garter snake.

Frozen Rodents

Pet stores that sell snakes often stock frozen rodents in a variety of sizes. If you choose to feed your garter snake pinkies, you should consider using frozen pinkies. They are convenient—you can buy a small supply and use them as needed—inexpensive, and more humane than feeding live mice. Before feeding, make sure the pinky is completely thawed out by setting it out on a plate for a few hours. Frozen pinkies will keep for about three months, so don't purchase too large a supply.

When they are young and in a stage of rapid growth, garter and ribbon snakes will need extra amounts of vitamin D3 and calcium, both of which are necessary for proper skeletal formation. Dust two meals each week in a powder mixed at two parts calcium to one part D3. Adult specimens (animals over 18 months old) require only one calcium/D3-dusted meal per week. Remember that a dusted meal is just that, dusted in only a faint covering of powder. Powder that is caked on or laid on thick is excessive and can be detrimental to your snake.

Feeding Amount and Frequency

A final aspect of captive feeding is the schedule. How much should you feed your garter snake? How often? In the wild, garter and ribbon snakes feed whenever the opportunity presents itself. Of course, that opportunistic habit is offset by periods of famine. The snake is too slow to catch the minnow, a frog sees the approaching garter snake and dives to safety, the farmer has poisoned his fields to kill pests so the garter snake must search elsewhere for prey, etc. In the captive environment, prey cannot escape and if feeding opportunities are presented too often, the snake risks growing obese. Juvenile garter and ribbon snakes, therefore, should be fed at least two to three times each week. Small, nutrient-rich meals should occur often, as very young snakes are in a stage of rapid growth, and they will need all the nourishment they can get. Larger, adult specimens need not be fed so frequently. One feeding every five to six days is sufficient.

Tricky Feeding

Sometimes a garter snake will not feed on prey that is dusted in vitamin/calcium powder; the flavor of the powder can be less than appetizing. Conquer this problem by hand-feeding your snake an earthworm or minnow. After the snake has begun swallowing one end of the prey, sprinkle a light dusting on the back half of the worm or minnow. A hungry garter snake will seldom reject a meal—even a dusted meal—once it has begun feeding.

Many hobbyists skirt the issue by housing their garter snake in a vivarium that has a running, cycling aquarium component to it—a living pond built into one half of the terrarium. The hobbyist simply keeps the pond half of the terrarium well-stocked with fish, salamanders, and tadpoles, replacing the feeders as the garter snake eats them. This approach to garter snake feeding is somewhat negligent and lazy on the part of the keeper, and may not supply sufficient nutrients to ensure the long-term health of the snake. If used in close conjunction with more varied food items and vitamin/mineral supplements, however, the pond-half method can work, and it can also make for some interesting viewing, allowing you to witness your garter snake slinking up to the edge of the pool and stalking the unsuspecting minnows, just as he would in the wild.

Breeding Garter
and Ribbon
Snakes

I think Jeff Goldblum said it best in *Jurassic Park:* "Scientists were so busy asking the question 'Could we [breed dinosaurs]?' that they didn't stop to ask, 'Should we?' " Too many hobbyists see the breeding of their pets as the high-water mark of a captive reptile endeavor, without stopping to consider the ramifications of that breeding. Will you be able to condition your breeders well enough that they survive the ordeal? What will you do with the offspring once they arrive? Do you have a safe, humane, and ecologically sound way of distributing the young? Irresponsible breeding projects result in either the death of the young (the hobbyist may release them in an ecosystem in which they cannot survive), or the demise of the ecosystem itself (a hobbyist releases the offspring in an area that cannot resist their adaptations, and the young out-compete the local fauna for food and water).

Captive breeding projects are best left to those of us who go in with a game plan. It is important to ask yourself some serious, realistic questions about the project and arrive at logical, well thought out answers about dealing with the young. Can you provide ample space and food for so many snakes, and maintain a high standard of living for all these new reptiles? If you can, then perhaps you are ready to take the first steps in the captive propagation of your pets.

Sexing

The beginning of any successful breeding project is the coupling of opposite sexes. Try as we may, our pet garters Betty and Victor will simply never breed if Victor is really Victoria! Determining the sex, therefore, of your snakes is the first critical step. Fortunately, this is done with relative ease. All male *Thamnophis* have a long tail that tapers gradually after the cloaca. Females, on the other hand, have a very abruptly tapering tail, which is much shorter than a male's. When comparing several snakes of the same size and age, it should be readily apparent which ones are the long-tailed males and which

Careful Probing

Probing to determine the sex of your garter/ribbon snakes is a delicate art to say the least. A metallic probe in the hands of a novice can do irreversible harm to the cloaca and genitalia of the probed snake. Anyone who has never before probed a snake should consult an expert to learn how this delicate act is properly performed. A responsible hobbyist will always put the health of his or her snake at the top of their priorities, and should never attempt to probe the animal unless certain how to do so. A herp veterinarian or snake-breeding friend should be able to show you how.

You must make sure your breeding pair is in excellent condition before cooling them. A gravid red-sided garter is pictured.

are the short-tailed females. If visual sexing is not possible (as is often true of juveniles), then probing may be necessary. Probing consists of sliding the blunt tip of a thin, metal rod inside the opening of the cloaca and gently pushing backward until the probe hits resistance. If the resistance comes after only three to five subcaudal scales, the specimen is female. If the probe goes on to pass eight to ten subcaudals, then you have a male.

Conditioning

Once you are certain that you have a pair of snakes, you'll want to make sure they are of breeding age and in good health. Garter and ribbon snakes (all species) do not attain sexual maturity until they are at least 18 months old. To ensure the long-term health of the snakes, breeding projects should be postponed until the animals are at least 22 to 24 months old, as breeding these snakes too early in life can shorten their life expectancy significantly; this is especially true of females. You'll also want to consider the health of the specimens in question. If your female snake is underweight or just recovering from a bout with internal parasites, she is not in any condition to bear young. Breeding females must be in peak health (proper weight, no diseases, etc.), as the carrying and bearing of young is a heavy burden on the female snake.

If you've come this far, you're well on your way to a successful breeding project. The next step is the preconditioning phase. Garter and ribbon snakes naturally enter their reproductive cycles in the early spring, soon after emerging from a long winter's sleep. Simulate this cycle by wintering your snakes in a cool, dark, quiet place at temperatures between 50° and 56°F. Before wintering them, (around late October) you'll want to feed your breeders several large meals, each supplemented with a dusting of calcium/D3 powder. This nutritious feast will help your snakes maintain good health during the winter. The extra calcium will also charge up the female's body, aiding her in supplying ample calcium and nutrients to her brood when they develop inside her.

Allow your snakes to fully digest and pass these final meals, then, by mid-November, you'll want to place your snakes in a dark, quiet place, like the basement of your house or in a seldom-used closet. Place the snakes in separate enclosures, lower the air temperature to 50° to 56°F, and discontinue feeding altogether. During this time, your snakes' metabolism will radically slow down, their movements will become fewer and fewer, and their bodies will enter a state known as brumation, which is best described as a form of incomplete hibernation.

As your snakes brumate, you'll want to check on them periodically. Remove them from their respective enclosures, inspect their bodies for sores or lesions which may have developed, and make sure their body mass/weight is still high. During the three to four months that your snakes will brumate, I recommend inspecting them at least once every three weeks. While no feeding occurs during brumation, it is important that you leave a dish of clean water in your snakes' enclosures at all times.

Breeding and Birth

Then, around the first week in March, remove your snakes from their brumating quarters, return them to ambient temperatures and photoperiod (73° to 79°F and 12 to 14 hours of daylight), and allow them to wake up, a process which could take several days. When your snakes emerge from their dormancy, their metabolism spikes, and their hormonal systems kick-in with a vengeance, driving the snakes to feed and seek mates.

Feed both the male and the female garter or ribbon snake as many times as they will eat over the next ten days, making sure to supplement every third meal with a dusting of calcium/D3 powder. Your female may go through a post-brumation shed, a key indicator that she is entering her ovulatory cycle, and that she is ready to mate. Introduce the two snakes by placing the male into the female's enclosure. Any short, quick, jerky motions on his part are good signs that he senses the female and is interested in mating with her. The two will slither side by side, intertwine their bodies, align their cloacas, and the male will insert his hemipene into the female's cloaca.

After two weeks, separate the two snakes. Resume feeding and maintaining the male as normal, but put the female on an accelerated feeding schedule. Feed her as often as she will eat, adding calcium/D3 supplements to every third meal. As the weeks roll by, the female will continue to eat and her mid-body will swell with the gestating young. At 12 weeks or so, you can expect to be the

Baby garter and ribbon snakes, like this red-sided garter neonate, are small animals that need a steady supply of appropriately sized prey.

Breeding Garter and Ribbon Snakes

proud "parent" of a new crop of bouncing baby garter or ribbon snakes! All garter and ribbon snakes bear their young alive but are not likely to give birth while anyone is around to see it. Make sure the female's enclosure is outfitted with plenty of deep, dark hide boxes to accommodate her need for privacy and seclusion during this delicate time.

Food Supply

Be aware that newborn garter and ribbon snakes are *very* small, and they will require specialty foods that may be difficult to obtain. Before attempting to breed your garters or ribbons, makes certain that you'll have a definite source for minnow and guppy fry, slices of earthworm, and tiny tadpoles for feeding the newborn snakes once they arrive.

Garter snakes are very prolific, producing more young than any other species of snake. A healthy brood may consist of 25 to 50 young, with 60 to 80 not uncommonly occurring in the broods of large, healthy female eastern garter snakes. Ribbon snakes typically bear smaller clutches of 10 to 22 young. Young need to be placed in individual enclosures soon after birth. Deli cups outfitted with white paper towel substrate, plenty of (tiny) ventilation holes, and a small dish of water make excellent and inexpensive housing for the plethora of young.

Young, which are also called neonates, will not eat until after they have shed their skin for the first time (called the post-natal shed), which will occur 6 to 10 days after birth. Feed neonates on tiny guppies; the smell and activity will entice the newborns' hunting instincts. Cut-up bits of earthworm, very small tadpoles, and tiny strips of supplemented fish will also be greedily accepted. Feed young as often as they will accept food. Add calcium/D3 supplement to every other meal, but add full-spectrum vitamin supplement only to every fourth meal. Maintain neonates at temperatures of 77° to 80°F.

Health
Care

The garter and ribbon snakes, like most colubrid snake species, are hardy by nature and are highly resistant to diseases. Resistant, however, does not mean immune. Their strong constitutions cannot stave off all illnesses, especially if the snake is housed in filthy or overly cold conditions. Ultimately, it is the responsibility of a conscientious keeper to provide both clean and warm living conditions, as well as regular veterinary checkups for his or her pet garter or ribbon snake.

No matter what disease your snake may contract, his recovery hinges on your hospital tank, or quarantine tank. Outfit sparsely with white paper towels and a single hide so that you may observe your animal at all times. Because they are cold-blooded, garter snakes will need some extra warmth when they are ailing. Basically the equivalent of a sick human running a low-grade fever, a little added warmth will help your snake's immune and metabolic systems to function at peak levels, thereby accelerating the reptile's rate of recovery. Maintain the hospital tank at two to three degrees higher than the snake's usual terrarium, though not to exceed an ambient temperature of 84°F, with a basking spot of not more than 89°F.

Act Healthy or Be Eaten

Garter and ribbon snakes, like most reptiles and amphibians, seldom show symptoms of illness during its early stages. In the wild, this is a survival tactic employed to help the ailing snake elude would-be predators, but in captivity, this resilience to appearing sick can mask the snake's ailment from the keeper until the disease is in its most advanced stages. The conscientious keeper must always be aware of the health of his or her snake, so that no symptoms go unnoticed and no disease goes untreated until it is too late.

External Parsites
Ticks

Most often seen on imported or wild-caught reptiles, external parasites may appear as either ticks or mites. Round, quarter-inch long, brown, reddish, or black "flaps" are reptilian ticks. These minuscule bloodsuckers appear as fleshy protuberances or flaps, and attach to the snake where the scales are thinnest and where the blood flow is great: near the head, eyes, mouth, and cloaca. Using their powerful jaws, the ticks bore through the skin of the snake and feed until they are fat and full.

Remove ticks by swabbing the parasite with a dab of petroleum jelly or mineral oil. Let the jelly sit atop the tick for about two hours, smothering it to death. After two hours, grasp the tick with a pair of tweezers and slowly pull the tick off. By applying gentle, even tension, you can usually remove the tick whole. Never jerk the tick, or pull suddenly, as this is likely to break the tick's body in half, leaving the head and mandibles attached to the snake. Retained

Mites often collect in the groove between the eye and the scales around it. Wandering garter snake pictured.

heads will almost certainly become infected, and will require veterinary treatment. Once you've plucked all the ticks, conclude treatment by applying a dab of topical antibiotic cream to the spot of attachment.

Mites

The second type of external parasite presents far more serious problems in the home terrarium. Perhaps the most insidious of all parasites, the mites are tiny, ravenous bloodsuckers that infest your snake's body, lay eggs in the terrarium's substrate, and reproduce to plague proportions in a matter of weeks. Appearing as black or reddish pepper-flecks crawling all over your garter snake, mites occur in large numbers (only a few mites can reproduce to over a thousand in a matter of a few weeks). They can drain a snake, especially a small snake, of a considerable amount of blood, thereby sapping his energy, lowering his hydration levels, and weakening his immune system. The incessant itching and burning of a mite infestation also causes the afflicted snake a great deal of pain and stress. If your snake is to survive, you must obliterate the invaders quickly and thoroughly to prevent future outbreaks. Steps for combating a mite infestation are as follows:

1. Remove the afflicted garter or ribbon snake from his terrarium.

2. Bathe the animal in lukewarm water, massaging the scales and washing away as many mites as possible.

Health Care

3. Place bathed snake in quarantine.

4. Dispose of all organic and non-cleanable substrate and décor in the infested terrarium. Tie up the garbage bag and take outside immediately.

5. Wash all inorganic environs (large rocks, hides, water dishes etc.) in *soapy, scalding-hot water* mixed with about 10 percent bleach.

6. Scald the terrarium with the soapy water and bleach, making sure to wash every little crack and corner, as mites will take refuge around the top and at the seams. Rinse well.

To treat the snake himself there are a number of options. You can spray the hostpital tank with Provent-A-Mite and then place the snake in the cage. As of this writing, this product appears to be safe to use in all snakes and lizards and is an effective mite-killer. Another way to dispose of mites on the snake himself is to give him a bath in lukewarm solution of water and povidone-iodine (available in drug stores). Make the solution dilute—the solution should be the color of weak tea. Change the water several times, and make sure the snake is completely submerged a few times— obviously, do not drown him.

When the infestation is over, rebuild your snake's home terrarium with all new substrate and clean décor. You may have to treat for mites two or three times; they are very persistent. It will make less work for you if you keep your snake in a minimalist cage until you are sure the mites are gone.

Internal Parasites

Internal parasites (worms, flukes, nematodes, etc.) are seldom problematic in captive-bred specimens and are associated with wild-caught or imported snakes. Symptoms of internal parasites include loss of appetite, unexplained and rapid weight loss (despite a healthy appetite), runny or mucus-laden stool, intensely sweet smelling stool, chronic vomiting, and listlessness. Because internal parasites are virtually impossible to diagnose outside of a medical lab, the

Pest Strips

Until recently, the standard mite treatment was to use vapona-impregnated insect-killing strips. However, more and more evidence is accumulating that these strips can cause death or injury in herps, sometimes many months after they have been used. It is probably best to avoid using them.

average hobbyist should never attempt to diagnose or treat internal parasites without first consulting a veterinarian. Once your vet identifies and diagnoses the problem, he or she can prescribe a treatment regimen that will put your snake back on the road to good health.

Injuries

Sores and lesions associated with injury can easily be treated with a topical antibiotic cream. If your snake is bitten, scraped, or if he rubs his nose raw on a screen lid, you need only wash the wound with fresh, clean water, disinfect by applying a cotton swab soaked in hydrogen peroxide, and apply a small dab of topical antibiotic cream to the affected area. Larger wounds, such as burns or severe cuts, require immediate veterinary attention.

Blister Disease

Blister disease occurs when your garter or ribbon snake is made to live in excessively moist or filthy conditions. Feces-laden substrate, urine-rich drinking water, high humidity, and poor ventilation are all possible causes of blister disease. As its name suggests, blister disease is a condition that affects the skin of your snake, causing the scales to blister, canker, and rot. Afflicted specimens may bear twisted, gnarled belly scales and patches of severe discoloration. An excruciatingly painful disorder, blister disease will, if left untreated, eventually spread deep into the muscle tissue of your garter snake, causing irreversible muscle and nerve damage. Once this happens, the demise of your pet is not far off.

Treat blister disease by removing your pet to the hospital tank, raising the ambient temperature to 81° to 82° Fahrenheit, lowering the relative humidity to less than 60 percent, and applying a topical antibiotic cream to the afflicted areas of the snake. Severe cases of blister disease (those in which the blisters have burst, leaving deep, pus-filled sores) call for immediate veterinary care and antibiotic injections. Your snake will enter a rapid shed cycle, which is a natural defense mechanism against blister disease diet. After several sheds, your snake will have replaced his old, damaged scales with fresh, new scales. Avoid future bouts of blister disease by maintaining a scrupulously clean and properly ventilated habitat for your snake.

Mouth Rot

Perhaps the most common ailment to afflict garter and ribbon snakes is mouth rot. Technically known as infectious stomatitis, this is a

Finding a Herp Vet

It is not always easy to find vets who are experienced with reptiles and amphibians. In rural areas, it may be impossible to find one within a reasonable distance. Here are some suggestions to help you locate a vet who can help with your pet snake. It is best if you locate one before you actually have an emergency

- Call veterinarians listed as "exotic" or "reptile" vets in the phonebook. Ask them questions to be sure they are familiar with garter and ribbon snakes.

- Ask at your local pet stores to see if there is someone they can recommend.

- Ask local zoos and animal shelters for a recommendation.

- Herpetological societies are likely to know which local vets treat reptiles and amphibians.

- Contact the Association of Reptilian and Amphibian Veterinarians. Their website is www.arav.org.

Although most garters and ribbons, including the coastal garter, frequent wet habitats in nature, an overly damp terrarium can lead to blister disease.

condition in which the mouth of the snake becomes infected by degenerative bacteria and possibly fungus. Brought about by unsanitary housing and low temperatures, mouth rot is extremely painful to the snake and, if left untreated, may be fatal. Symptoms include the formation of cheesy, yellowish exudate in the mouth, the blackening and falling-out of the teeth, and inflammation of the gums. Treat mouth rot by removing to quarantine the afflicted snake and raising the ambient temperature in the terrarium by two to three degrees. *Gently* pry open your snake's mouth and clear away the cheesy material with a moist cotton swab. Soak a second swab in an iodine or hydrogen peroxide solution and dab the afflicted areas of the mouth. Repeat this process daily until all inflammation and exudate disappears. You stand the best chance of successfully combating this disease if you seek veterinary treatment.

Respiratory Diseases

Respiratory diseases stem from cold or excessively humid conditions, and signs include sneezing, wheezing, snorting, labored breathing, and holding the mouth agape. Much akin to a respiratory infection in humans, this condition is far worse in garter and ribbon snakes, as these animals only have one functioning lung and can succumb quickly to infection. If you suspect your snake has or is developing a respiratory infection, seek veterinary care immediately, as this ailment is easily cured with the proper medical treatment. If left unchecked, however, even a seemingly mild respiratory infection may worsen and prove fatal in a surprisingly short length of time.

Most illnesses of pet snakes are caused by poor husbandry: poor diet, infrequent cleaning, improper temperature, and improper humidity. Eastern ribbon snake pictured.

Digestive Disorders

Sometimes brought about by eating tainted foods, digestive tract disorders may also occur if the snake is kept at temperatures insufficient to sustain proper digestion. As the meal sits in the snake's belly undigested, it will begin to rot and quickly poison the snake's systems. In most cases, the snake will regurgitate the meal, but sometimes a bacterial infection will take hold in the snake's digestive tract, which can lead to serious health problems. Always maintain sufficiently warm temperatures inside your snake's terrarium, with a basking spot of 85° to 87° F. If your snake does seem to fall ill after regurgitating a meal, seek veterinary care at once for diagnosis and treatment.

Gut Impactions

One type of digestive disorder is known as the impacted gut. When your garter or ribbon snake feeds, he may ingest tiny grains of substrate along with his meal. Organic bits of matter (shreds of bark, grains of peat, etc.) often pass through the snake's system with no ill effects. Inorganic matter, however, may clog your snake's intestines, leading to bloating, swelling, and a slow and painful death. For this reason, you should never house your garter or ribbon snake atop decorative glass beads, aquarium pebbles, sand, or other small, inorganic matter. A healthy garter snake will pass his meal within three to four days after eating. If you feed your snake and notice that he is not passing any meals, then an impacted gut may be to blame. Seek the care of a veterinarian immediately. If caught early (usually via x-rays), an impacted gut may be remedied without surgery. If the blockage is too severe, however, surgery is the only way to save the snake's life.

Species, Subspecies, and Color Morphs

As one might expect from a group of snakes as common and widespread as the ribbon and garter snakes, these animals are represented in the pet trade by a wide variety of species. Selective breeding projects supply the ever-growing pet trade with popular varieties of garter and ribbon snakes without depleting natural populations through the wild collecting of snakes. While there are far more species of garter and ribbon snakes than can be covered in a book like this one, I have listed several species that you are likely to encounter in the pet shop. Once you've got a good idea of what species of garter or ribbon snake you want to keep, I urge you, my readers, to educate yourself as best you can on that particular species. Learn all you can about it and the nuances of its particular needs in captivity, so that both you and your snake may benefit from a long and joyous keeper-kept relationship.

Butler's Garter Snake

The Butler's garter snake, *T. butleri*, is a quietly attractive serpent, wearing a base coat of brownish to black, with three distinct yellowish stripes running from immediately behind the head to the tip of the tail. One stripe runs along the midline of the back, while two others flank either side of the body. Rows of black spots may or may not be faintly visible between the yellow stripes. Growing to a maximum length of 26 inches, the Butler's garter snake thrives naturally in open meadows, low-lying grasslands, swamp borderlands, streamside forests, and marshes throughout eastern Ontario, Michigan, Indiana, and parts of Ohio. Because of his small stature and benign disposition, the Butler's garter snake makes a peaceable, even-tempered pet. It should be noted, however, that these snakes may not adapt well to captivity, often times refusing to feed. Fussy feeders may be coaxed into eating when offered small salamanders or leeches, both of which are available at most bait shops or from specialty retailers online. Earthworms are perhaps the favorite food of the Butler's garter snake. House Butler's garters at temperatures of 72° to 78°F and relative humidity of no less than 65 percent. Captive-bred individuals seldom refuse food.

Black-Necked Garter Snake

Hailing from the mesquite deserts of western Texas, west to central Arizona, north into Colorado and south all the way into Guatemala, the black-necked garter snake, *T. cyrtopsis*, grows to 20 to 42 inches long. Sporting a ground color of olive-gray to pale orange, the black-necked garter snake wears three dorsolateral stripes of yellow to orange. As you might deduce from his common name, this species is distinguished by two black, egg-shaped blotches located directly behind the jaws on either side of the neck at the base of the skull. Two alternating rows of black spots are frequently visible between the yellow-orange body stripes.

Black-necked garter snakes are divided into three subspecies: western *(T. c. cyrtopsis)*, eastern *(T. c. ocellatus)*, and southern *(T. c. fulvus)*. Depending on which subspecies you own, housing requirements may be slightly different; *T. c. fulvus* requires slightly higher levels of humidity than does either of the other subspecies. Make sure you know which subspecies

The western black-necked garter snake is found from Utah and Colorado to Guatemala. An eastern black-necked garter is pictured at the start of the chapter.

you are dealing with before making purchase. Wild-caught black-necked garter snakes often suffer from heavy parasite loads and should be examined by your veterinarian immediately after purchase.

Fond of desert highlands, rocky outcroppings, and streamside fir forests, the black-necked garter snake must be housed in a warm, relatively dry environment. Temperatures of 74° to 80°F with a basking spot of 85° to 88°F and relative humidity of not more than 60 percent. This species is fond of tadpoles and small frogs, though minnows and earthworms are typically accepted in captivity as well. The black-necked garter snake is also fond of early morning basking, so a captive specimen should receive no less than six hours of basking opportunity each day. After warming to its optimal body temperature, this species will retreat into a dark hideaway. Employ plenty of ground cover and hides in the black-necked garter's terrarium.

Western Terrestrial Garter Snake

The western terrestrial garter snake, *T. elegans*, is a hardy, robust animal whose earthen ground colors and subdued stripes grant this snake excellent camouflage when hiding amidst the grasses and sand flats of his homeland. Growing to a maximum of 42 inches, the western terrestrial garter occurs in four subspecies: the mountain garter snake, *T. e. elegans*; the coast garter snake, *T. e. terrestris*; the wandering garter snake, *T. e. vagrans*; and the San Pedro Martir garter snake, *T. e. hueyi*. All subspecies of *T. elegans* may, however, be successfully housed at temperatures of 72° to 78°F with a basking spot of 85° to 88°F and relative humidity of 55 to 65 percent. Terrestrial garters also require plenty of thick ground cover. Preferred food items include all the standard fare, but terrestrial garters are one of the species that eat small lizards, birds, and baby rodents whenever possible. Adults specimens do well if supplied with the occasional lizard, bird, or mammal in captivity.

Checkered Garter Snake

The checkered garter snake, *T. marcianus*, is one of the few snake species that is actually benefiting from the expansion of mankind.

Aquatic Garters

Though they are seldom encountered on the open market, the so-called aquatic garter snakes comprise a large subgroup of garter snakes. Comprised of five species and subspecies, this group of garters includes the Santa Cruz aquatic garter, *T. atratus atratus*; the Oregon aquatic garter, *T. a. hydrophilus*; the two-striped garter, *T. hammondi*; the Sierra garter, *T. couchi*; and the giant garter snake, *T. gigas*, which may grow to nearly 58 inches long, making him easily the longest and most heavy-bodied of all the garter snakes. Found throughout coastal California and parts of Baja, Nevada, and Oregon, the aquatic garter snakes feed primarily on salamanders, leeches, and minnows, but have unusually short life expectancies; even the healthiest specimens seldom exceed seven to eight years old.

The two-striped and the other species in the aquatic garter snake group are seldom offered for sale.

As more and more arid desert land is converted to irrigated farmland, the range of the checkered garter snakes is expanding into the new, manmade habitat. Taking his common name from the dark checkerboard pattern on his back, the checkered garter wears a base coat of sandy brown to straw yellow. Perhaps the most easily tamed of all the garters, this species is very docile indeed. Even wild-caught adults tame with gentle handling within a few days of capture. House at 76° to 80° with a basking spot of 85° and a large water dish. Plenty of stony ground cover is advised, and artificial cave hide boxes work well for this species. A heavy-bodied animal, the checkered garter may grow to 41 inches, though most specimens do not exceed 34 inches. Fish and tadpoles comprise the lion's share of the diet, while small rodents should occasionally be offered to large adult specimens. Captive breeding projects involving the checkered garter snake almost always meet with high success rates. Winter for three to four months prior to mating, which occurs in nature from April to May. Gestation lasts roughly three months, with 12 to 20 babies in the usual litter. Young are very hardy, eat well, and grow quickly. Albino forms of the checkered garter snake are frequently encountered in the pet trade.

Species, Subspecies, and Color Morphs

Common Garter Snake

The flagship species of *Thamnophis*, the common garter, *T. sirtalis*, is, and has been for over half a century, the most popularly kept snake in the world. Commanding high prices throughout Europe and Japan, this demure little serpent has won the hearts of hobbyists worldwide. Occurring in nature from Ontario east to the Atlantic and south through Florida, the common garter snake, or one of his subspecies, occurs in all 48 contiguous states, making him the most wide-ranging species in North America.

Same Snake, Different Name

 The common garter snake is sometimes known as the eastern garter snake—even those subspecies found in the western part of the range. To make matters more complicated, one subspecies, *T. sirtalis sirtalis*, is also called the eastern garter snake. So, the term "eastern garter snake" can refer to just the eastern subspecies or to the species as a whole. It is less confusing to use the term "eastern garter snake" just for *T. sirtalis sirtalis*, and use the term "common garter snake" for all the subspecies together.

The common garter is one of the largest of the garter snakes, and may grow to a whopping 52 inches long. Despite his impressive size, however, the common garter makes an excellent pet (hence, this animal's popularity). Found around marshes, wetlands, meadows, pine forests, farms, ditches, and hardwood groves, the eastern garter is recognized by well-defined back and side stripes, between which there often occur alternating rows of black blotches. Frequently, there are red interstitial (between the scales) markings.

The common garter snake may be housed at temperatures of 76° to 80°F with a basking spot of 83° to 85°F. Employ large waters dishes, and feed a varying diet of earthworms, minnows, goldfish, salamanders, tadpoles, and the occasional small frog to large adult specimens.

Red-Sided Garter Snake

The red-sided garter, *T. s. parietalis*, is one of the more attractive snakes in the hobby. Hailing from British Columbia and Saskatchewan southeast to Oklahoma, this species wears a contrasting coat of dark brown to black, a bright yellow-green back stripe, and evenly spaced bars of red adorning his flanks. The head is bright red, and the belly is greenish-blue with black spots. The red-sided garter snake needs plenty of vegetative ground cover—mosses, ferns, hollow logs, hides, etc.—and he also seems to relish a few hours of early morning basking atop flat rocks and broad branches. Minnows and earthworms are the preferred food items.

Blue-Striped Garter Snake

A southern subspecies of the common garter, the blue-striped garter snake, *T. s. similis*, is aptly named, as his belly, flanks, and side

Blue-striped garter snakes are remarkably similar to blue-striped ribbon snakes, and the two occur in the same natural range.

Species, Subspecies, and Color Morphs

stripes are bright blue. Growing to a maximum length of just under 40 inches, the blue garter is one of the more aquatic species and is seldom encountered far from a source of permanent water. House at temperatures of 78° to 81°F and at relative humidity no less than 65 percent. Incorporating plenty of artificial vegetation (vines and other arboreal plants) and large hunks of driftwood will simulate this species' natural environment, while at the same time accommodate their need to climb and wander. Large adults favor frogs, tadpoles, and salamanders as prey.

San Francisco Garter Snake

Ask any fan of the garter snakes which species is at the top of their list, and you're very likely to hear "the San Francisco garter" as a reply. The magnificently colored San Francisco garter, *T. s. tetrataenia*, is a subspecies of the common garter snake, and is considered *extremely endangered,* as its natural range is only San Mateo County, California. Wearing stripes of blue, black, and red with a greenish-blue belly and crimson head, the San Francisco garter is perhaps the finest jewel of the garter and ribbon snakes.

One of the most endangered garter snakes is also one of the most beautiful: the San Francisco garter.

These snakes, though bred in some numbers in captivity every year, seldom appear on the pet trade. When they do come up for purchase, they always command a very high price. This animal is protected under State of California laws, as well as under federal wildlife protection laws, so harvesting one from the wild is certainly not an option.

Western Ribbon Snake

Instantly distinguishable from the garter snakes by their thin frames and exceedingly long tails (which may comprise more than 30 percent of the total body length), the ribbon snakes occur on the pet trade in three major varieties. The western ribbon snake, *T. proximus*, ranges from the Mississippi Valley north to Wisconsin, west to central New Mexico, and south to Costa Rica, and wears a rather bland coat of dark brown to tan accented with well-defined back and side stripes of pale yellow to deep orange. Large adults rarely exceed three feet in length. Because of his wide range, the western ribbon snake may be housed in a variety of habitats, so it's good to know exactly which geographic area your snake comes from, especially if he is an imported or wild-caught specimen. House according to your pet's natural environs. Employ plenty of branches, arboreal vegetation, vines, and other climbable items, as well as one or more large water dishes, in the western ribbon snake's habitat. Captive fare primarily includes fish and tadpoles.

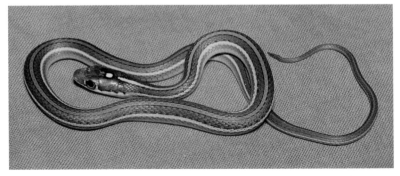

The red-striped ribbon snake is found throughout much of Texas and just enters Mexico.

Species, Subspecies, and Color Morphs

Eastern ribbon snakes require a large water bowl or a half-land and half-water setup in captivity.

Eastern Ribbon Snake

The eastern ribbon snake, *T. sauritus*, grows only slightly larger than his western cousin, frequently attaining lengths of 28 to 38 inches. Dorsal coloration is dark brown to black base with three, well-defined stripes of yellow to off-white or cream along the flanks and midline of the back. Found throughout all of the eastern United States, except in northern New England, the eastern ribbon snake thrives in habitats surrounding large bodies of water. Employing several large water dishes or constructing a living vivarium with at least one-third of the floor space being water is definitely recommended. Eastern ribbon snakes also enjoy hanging in and slithering through arboreal perches, so plenty of lofty décor is in order, including vines, climbs, branches, etc. Eastern ribbon snakes, though priced cheaply on the open market, may present problems feeding in the captive environment, often refusing all fare other than minnows and tadpoles.

Blue-Striped Ribbon Snake

By far the most attractive member of the ribbon snake group, the blue-striped ribbon snake, *T. s. nitae*, wears a base coat of ebony black accented by three sky blue stripes adorning the flanks and centerline of the back. The belly is also bright blue. Found along the gulf coast of Florida, from Wakulla County to the Withlacoochee River, this species faces endangerment as paved streets and cleared land expands. Fortunately, these snakes have been embraced by herp hobbyists, so captive-breeding projects supply the lion's share of specimens to the pet market. House blue-striped ribbon snakes as you would the eastern ribbon snake, making sure to provide plenty of foliage and ground cover. These animals feed on a variety of fare, and are usually the boldest of all the ribbon snakes when it comes to feeding in captivity. Many specimens have to be fed with tongs for fear of them biting their keepers. Feed them primarily fish and tadpoles, augmented with earthworms, salamanders, and the occasional pinkie mouse. Blue-striped ribbon snakes are prized not only for their unusual, azure beauty, but also for their hardy nature and gentle demeanor; they are perhaps the most handle-friendly of all the ribbon snakes.

Blue-striped ribbon snakes are found in a small range on the northwestern coast of Florida.

Color Variants

Albino variants of various garter snake species have been on the market for several years now, and they are becoming more readily available to the average enthusiast. By definition, an albino creature is one lacking or deficient in pigmentation. While some of these animals may retain some degree of yellow pigment, most are still referred to as albino.

Species, Subspecies, and Color Morphs   61

In the herp hobby, the term *albino* is usually used inter-changeably with *amelanistic*, which is the lack of the black pigment melanin. Some of the more commonly en-countered varieties are the albino checkered garter snake

Albino individuals are found in many types of garter and ribbon snakes, including the red-sided garter (above) and the Gulf Coast ribbon snake.

and the albino eastern garter snake. Amelanistic terrestrial garters and red-sided garters are known, as well. These animals typically fetch a much higher price than their norm-ally colored brethren. Because albino specimens lack pro-tective pigmentation, they must not be exposed to UV light. Dark pigment protects

the cells and organs of all animals from the harmful rays of the sun; without pigmentation, these animals have absolutely no defense from sunlight or UV bulbs, and must never be exposed to either one.

There are also leucistic (white snakes usually with blue eyes) plains garter snakes, *T. radix*. Leucistic animals are typically more expensive than their albino counterparts, and they occur with less frequency on the pet trade. Selective breeding by herpetoculturist Dr. Phil Blais has resulted in an intensely red common garter known as the flame garter. As more and more private breeding projects occur, and as more and more people become interested in the garter and ribbon snakes, I'm sure that new and even more exciting color varieties will come about. With so many species and possibilities to choose from, who can say what amazing color morph will appear next?

Resources

MAGAZINES

Contemporary Herpetology
Southeastern Louisiana University
www.nhm.ac.uk/hosted_sites/ch

Herp Digest
www.herpdigest.org

Reptiles Magazine
P.O. Box 6050
Mission Viejo, CA 92690
www.animalnetwork.com/reptiles

ORGANIZATIONS

American Society of Ichthyologists and Herpetologists
Maureen Donnelly, Secretary
Grice Marine Laboratory
Florida International University
Biological Sciences
11200 SW 8th St.
Miami, FL 33199
Telephone: (305) 348-1235
E-mail: asih@fiu.edu
www.asih.org

Society for the Study of Amphibians and Reptiles (SSAR)
Marion Preest, Secretary
The Claremont Colleges
925 N. Mills Ave.
Claremont, CA 91711
Phone: 909-607-8014
E-mail: mpreest@jsd.claremont.edu
www.ssarherps.org

Amphibian, Reptile & Insect Association
Liz Price
23 Windmill Rd
Irthlingsborough
Wellingborough NN9 5RJ
England

List of Local Herp Societies
www.kingsnake.com/society.html

WEB RESOURCES

HerpNetwork
www.herpnetwork.com

Kingsnake
www.kingsnake.com

Kingsnake (UK)
www.kingsnake.co.uk

Alan Francis' Garter Snake Home Page
www.gartersnake.co.uk/index.htm

VETERINARY RESOURCES

Association of Reptile and Amphibian Veterinarians
P.O. Box 605
Chester Heights, PA 19017
Phone: 610-358-9530
Fax: 610-892-4813
E-mail: ARAVETS@aol.com
www.arav.org

RESCUE AND ADOPTION SERVICES

ASPCA
424 East 92nd Street
New York, NY 10128-6801
Phone: (212) 876-7700
E-mail: information@aspca.org
www.aspca.org

Petfinder
www.petfinder.org

RSPCA (UK)
Wilberforce Way
Southwater
Horsham, West Sussex RH13 9RS
Telephone: 0870 3335 999
www.rspca.org.uk

Index

Note: Boldface numbers indicate illustrations.

Measurement Conversion Chart

UNITS USED IN THIS BOOK
1 gallon = 3.7854 liters
1 inch = 2.54 centimeters
32°F = 0°C (water freezes)
75°F = 23.9°C

CONVERTING FAHRENHEIT TO CELSIUS
Subtract 32 from the Fahrenheit temperature.
Divide the answer by 9.
Multiply that answer by 5.

Photo Credits

W. B. Allen, Jr.: 17
R. D. Bartlett: 3, 27, 43, 45, 51
Jon Boxall: 34
Suzanne L.Collins: 58
Paul Freed: 32, 62 (bottom)
James E. Gerholdt: 10, 19, 62 (top)
W. P. Mara: 7, 15, 26, 29, 39, 41, 59
G & C. Merker: 1, 4, 5, 53
A. Norman: 57
M. Panzella: 13
Philip Purser: 21, 50, 60, 61
K. H. Switak: 49, 55
John Tyson: 14
Erika Weiss-Geissler: 37